MY WALK

DARRELL SOMERS

My Walk

Adriel Publishing

Cover artwork by Darrell Somers

Cover design by Darrell Somers & Elizabeth Lawless

ISBN: 979-8-9896554-0-3

THIS BOOK IS DEDICATED TO

MY FAMILY AND FRIENDS

WHO HAVE ALWAYS SUPPORTED ME

IN ALL MY ENDEAVORS.

THANKS FOR YOUR NEVER-ENDING

LOVE AND SUPPORT.

Table of Contents

Answers

The hope eternally.

Is to talk with the Savior True.

Right now, you have questions indefinitely.

Do you think the questions have answers that will give you a clue?

When you walk through the door to the unknown.

And the Deliverer stands with all that went before.

All the questions and hate will be laid at the throne.

Touching the robe gives all answers to the questions before.

Never be a doubting Thomas.

He will give eternally like his promise.

AWAKE

I am tired of this sleepwalk dance.

I don't want to leave this zombie walking state to chance.

I need something for my soul.

This sleepwalk dance is taking its toll.

Something that will let me soar high above the rainbow.

Numb my senses and make me glow.

Glow as bright as a harvest moon.

Get my mind and body dancing in tune.

Live my life with my eyes wide open.

Not just going day to day coping.

Awake from this sleepwalk dance!!!

BEAMS OF SOUND

I close my eyes and start falling into emptiness.

When my eyes open there are beams of colorfulness.

Where I am is not important to all that surround my soul.

All I feel is the beams of colors penetrating like hot coal.

Leaping for joy and never coming down I just exist in this nirvana.

Looking through a magnifying glass of this enlightenment and persona.

The sounds that surround me fall into deafness with each note I hear.

I dance and sing with every beam of color that penetrates my fear.

My mind becomes chaotic with every beat that raps on the drum.

Rapid eye movement makes me cherish my robust sum.

The music goes silent, and the beams of colors fade.

Back to truth, my eyes open, where all light is made.

No purple gum drop trees or beams that soar.

Every crook of my mind has been cut to the core.

Carefree and peaceful sounds slice me like a knife.

My world is in perfect harmony with the sounds that is my life.

Believe

I think about someone saying a prayer for the first time.

Praying to let your light shine.

I think about the day you became my guiding star.

How you have shown me so many things.

My mind finds it bizarre.

That I walk daily with the King of Kings.

Seems I'm always at a loss for what to do.

You are always close.

Even if I don't feel your presence come through.

Helping fight my daily struggles with foes.

There is something about your presence that moves me.

All my fears and anxiety flee.

Knowing I'm a sinner.

Thinking I must look for a God to pray too.

Not knowing, with you in my life I'm already a winner.

My Savior True.

BLOOD

When I am standing at the great unknown's
entrance.

Thinking back on the way I lived.

Will my faith be enough to gain entrance.

Will my sins block me for my struggles and strived.

Then I remembered that I always have that,
Champion.

I will let his blood speak for me.

For all the time I make the same mistakes.

I am guilty of not always being the best I could've
been.

There are millions of points of views.

Many learned people have different thoughts.

But for me there is only a simple thought.

Do I believe He Reigns?

Will His blood speak for me?

Coffee

The light of the day is shining in my eyes through my window.

The world is spinning in perfect harmony with my soul.

I awake to the sounds of nature and the smell of coffee.

This is another day that my heart can be renewed so I can be the person I should be.

My heart rejoices with the thought of being encircled by family and friends that care.

The red bird sings that song of hope so I leap from the bed dancing like no one else is there.

The transgressions of my past have been cleared just like the darkness to the morning light.

I can hold my head high throughout the day knowing the same will happen for tomorrows fight.

Being true to you and not worried about what others think they know, is the path set before us all.

The best part of the day is sitting outside in the silence listening to what is being said in natures call.

Harmonization with your surroundings knowing it is well with your soul.

Colors Of The Fire

The glow of the fire reviles past and present casting of my lots.

I am watching the embers of my life floating from the fire into the air.

Starring at the different colors in the fire sparks my memories of my life.

Some of the colors of the flames bring back memories I wished would burn out.

Most of the colors are vibrant and happy that makes me smile.

I see many faces in the glow that I wished were still here.

I miss every one of them as I reflect on the good times we shared.

The flames grow higher as I sit with good friends reminiscing about life.

Feeling sad that just like life the fire will slowly fade.

Excited that with every fire that burns it will spark memories in my mind.

Colors

Paint me in any color.

Try to keep me down with your restraint collar.

Without even knowing me, telling me what I can be.

In your mind you are better than me.

All the labels you try to put on me, just know you are wrong.

I am happiest being me, and not trying to spin your label song.

Your opinion of me doesn't affect me in the least. Knowing who I am and what I can do will keep me at Peace.

Being born into money and privilege doesn't make you superior.

The people I see that are the happiest don't meet that criteria.

Money might give you opportunity; you can't buy ethics or respect.

Judging and talking about others is the way to deflect.

Whatever your color is, be happy and let others be their own color.

DAILY WALK

While on my daily walk with the Savior True.

I asked was it hard for him to be tortured and die on the cross.

He smiled and said, "did I think it was hard for the sky to be blue"?

Did I think that it is hard for believers to confess him no matter the cost?

He said there will be what seems like insurmountable things in life.

But just like he said, let my Fathers will be done.

Trust that the pain you might feel is only temporary.

Know that one day you will be called home.

That day there will be rejoicing with no more pain.

You will be home with all who love you.

He said that the pain he might have felt was for me to meet the Father.

Just like the love and sacrifice of every parent for their children.

DAYDREAM

My eyes close and I am taken to a fantastic place.

I feel warm purple sunlight on my face.

As I glide through cotton candy trees.

The smell takes me back to when I was young and free.

The chocolate river flows like a fountain of happiness.

Sharp winds fly through my soul; I feel the warm winds briskness.

All the fur babies that I have known greet me with stuffed bear hugs.

My mind is filled with elation like a sweet licorice tug.

Pink hummingbirds buzz in my head.

My laughter fills the dream until all sorrow has fled.

All is right in this fantastic daydream.

Loved ones are near as I float downstream.

My only wish would be to stay in this daydream for just a moment longer.

END OF THE LINE

Let your light shine.

Living for the end of the line.

Be careful what you say.

Every day is Judgement Day.

Remember to live and let live.

So, your light will shine when you arrive.

At the end of the line.

Your mind and actions align.

Salvation is for all.

That will listen to the call.

At the end of the line.

Welcome my friend you did fine.

Eyes Open

Hard times are coming over the skyline.

Be careful what you sew in your timeline.

Look deep in your heart for compassion.

Don't criticize others for their opinion.

The world with all its loveliness.

Don't help with the ugliness.

Don't be blinded by false trust.

Leave this world a better place, not to the unjust.

FATHER TIME

There are times I still feel I have game.

Then my body reminds me I'm not the same.

My mind tries to prove my body wrong.

Unfortunately, my body sings a different song.

When I was young, I felt invincible.

Nowadays I just hope the aches are tolerable.

There will come a day you will realize.

That time flies.

Thinking back, there were wasted days.

But most were the best I have to say.

Time is something you need to cherish.

Father Time shows everything will perish.

FLAWLESS

Why are the answers you seek to shame?

You always are seeking ways to push the blame.

The answers you want to find are not truth.

It is easy going through life thinking everyone else talks untruth.

Looking in the mirror and knowing that everyone has flaws.

It's time to face your flaws and stand up for the right cause.

It's hard to swallow that pride.

Let your ethics instead of your pride be your guide.

What a dark path thinking you are perfection.

We all need family & friends that love all our imperfection.

Let's show love without an agenda of trying to be flawless.

FLAWS

Tell me why you always think you are smarter than all of creation?

You think whatever you do is with grace and perfection.

Just remember that trying to achieve flawlessness will never end well.

Tell me what you will say when you hear the toll of the bell.

The insults you spew are hurtful, but you pass them off as jokes.

You know how to get under other skins with abusive pokes.

Others think it's funny if you don't set your sites their way with a surgeon's scalpel.

You judge others that use these tactics of harassing others, it's just a baffle.

You can take it as well as dish it out but does that make it right.

I wished you would just take the time before it ends in a fight.

I am sending smoke signs to show you how your words can be a dagger to my soul.

FLY

Scared of the wind.

Staying where you are.

Always looking around.

To see what might be coming down.

Drowning in your fears.

Looking through the windows of your mind.

Trying to see what is on the other side.

Never try to open the door.

In the canyons of your mind.

To walk through to see what is holding you back.

Is it real or just voices in your mind.

Holding you prisoner.

If only you could spread your wings.

Fly away to a better place in your mind.

Just spread your wings and fly away.

Free Will

Look at the sky of blue.

To see the Savior True.

He will give you eternal hope.

He will help you cope.

It will be your choice.

He gives free will to hear his voice.

All sins can be forgiven

Through His blood that was given.

GIVE

Give a piece of your soul.

Show others they can reach their goals.

Look at the child with tears.

Give a little time to help calm their fears.

We only need to give a piece of ourselves.

So they can see the greatness in themselves.

Imagine a world where everyone only has opportunity.

Where there is only unity.

No hunger, no abuses only love and support.

Life is too short.

It's not hard to choose love and compassion.

GOODBYE

Sadness flows under the moonlit sky.

There are a million questions why.

My awareness soars through the mountain blue.

With my thoughts focused on me and you.

I am consumed with fear and loneliness.

All the while thinking of you brings me happiness.

Losing someone that you have loved is depressing.

They say time heals all wounds but right now it's overwhelming.

It is hard to know left from right or even if this is real.

I close my eyes sleep doesn't come it just feels surreal.

My mind races with questions of promises.

Do I really believe what I believe with reverences.

Trying to understand what lies beyond the unknown.

Knowing that your light shines bright for your path home.

I can hear your voice in the warm breeze through the trees.

I see your face in every beautiful painting of the seas.

You will always be near me as I remember your face.

Goodbye for now from our loving embrace.

Holier Than Thou

Sitting around and waiting for the end of the line.

Always expecting saving Grace all the time.

Never showing compassion with actions.

But always talking about how righteous during interactions.

Judging others and condemning for sin.

While hiding in a closet committing the same sin.

We are called to spread Jesus's word and love.

Not to Judge.

If a person rejects Jesus, they are not rejecting you.

Plant the seed of love not the seed of hate.

After the seed of love is planted, let Jesus cultivate.

I'M OK

When I die, please don't shed tears.

Take a moment and calm all your fears.

Know that I will miss you until we are together.

I am walking to the light, seeing loved ones altogether.

Know that when I said I Love You.

I meant it, so don't be blue.

Each time I said something that caused you pain.

It will be burnt eternally in my brain.

I will always remember how in love we were.

Our life together passed like a blur.

Know that I am OK, so keep living.

It Doesn't Matter

It doesn't matter what shoes you wear or car you drive.

When it's your time all that you have collected will be unavailable.

So it doesn't matter if you have riches or poverty-stricken.

We all will be in a place where worldly possession will not help you with your answers.

If you think you're better than someone wait until you are in front of your maker.

That person could be in front of you while waiting to enter the hereafter.

All the worldly possessions will not move you one step closer.

Make sure you are invested in what you give and with your actions instead of things that doesn't matter.

Be sure that when you are gone people will miss you and not what you obtained.

IT

Storm clouds in my mind.

The answers I try to find.

Will love come from it?

If not, let go of it.

Keep your mind free of it.

Never clutter your mind with it.

Always easy to say it.

Hard to free your mind from it.

JOURNEY

I will take a midnight ride down the river of life.

Let the calm waters take away all my strife.

In the middle of the night, I will take a plunge into the living water.

Arise and let the cleansing rejuvenate my soul like rose water.

As the droplets roll down my face.

I finally can see a magical place.

Reawakening with love filling my heart.

All the dissension that I have has fallen apart.

The water has released the chains that kept me down.

I will walk the trail of wake and leave all doubt that made me frown.

My journey starts by climbing the mountain of faith.

LAST JOURNEY

Throughout a life we prepare for taking journeys.

Scheduling transportation, time off, where to stay, and packing.

The most fantastic journey we will take has already been planned.

The last journey in a life we will not have to worry about the details.

All the pain and worries of this life will be washed away.

Like most journey's anticipation can make us nervous about what is next.

The arrival gives us peace so we can see all the beauty that waits.

Yes there will be loved ones left behind that will miss seeing you.

The thing about this sole journey is we all will make that Last Journey.

To be reunited with all who have went to the great unknown before us.

LEARN

My mind races the darkness of the night.

Where there is no light.

A shooting star comes into view.

I jumped on it and flew.

I see my past life.

There are many regrets and strife.

Not keeping love first.

Trying to climb the ladder was a curse.

For all deplorable things that I have done.

I deserve to be shunned.

Not giving love to all the love that I was given.

I can only hope that I am forgiven.

Knowing where I was yesterday.

Is not where I am today?

When being loved for who you are sounds sappy.

Money and possessions are a short-lived happy.

The hard part is having people enter my life then exit as fast.

But that moment in time they are indispensable in my past.

It is hard to know why they are not needed for what's yet to come.

I want to use what I learned from my past to shape my sum.

LIFE

Let's take a moon light stroll by calm waters and melt into the night.

Hold hands and just be one while we soar high as a kite in flight.

Ascending through the dark until night becomes day.

Surf the beams of daylight until we reach the clouds high and away.

Feel the warm winds that blow through our soul riding on the wings of down feather pillow.

We live through the sensation of the wheels of life turning while soaring high in the clouds that billow.

It might be a thousand years or it could be only one second but at that time we sense content.

Feeling joy as we soar to our ultimate descent.

Never worried about where we will land or when our flight will send us spiraling down.

Life tells us to reach higher than a rainbow trying to touch every color at the speed of sound.

Making our whole existence relaxed knowing that we are surrounded by marshmallow goodness.

Finally we are coming back down to earth as night begins to cover the daylights winds of happiness.

Our feet straddle the large steed of reality that gallops through our time on this sphere.

With every thought we know that we are on our path jumping the gaps with our family and peers.

We focus on living life to the fullest never forgetting the ones that have taken the journey of a life time.

LIGHT

Standing in the middle of the darkest rain.

Thinking this must be the greatest pain.

Looking out into the distance and seeing a sliver of light.

Wondering if this pain will be lifted by the bright light.

Out of the darkness comes the voices of true believers.

The dark becomes light that silences my minds non-believers.

While Truth Reigns, Darkness will have no power or chains.

Holy Holy the True Redeemer Reigns.

LOST

My mind goes to a country road with blue skies and cool breezes.

Sitting in the back seat with the top down looking at your beautiful soul hoping time freezes.

Knowing that our time together is fleeting as the miles pass by, my heart is filled with elation.

You are my light that brightens my path as I walk through life with no hesitation.

We feel we lost you too early in this life but, I see your face at ease with no suffering.

Without saying a word, the smile on your radiant face tells me everything is pleasing.

I want to ask you so many things, but all I want in this moment is just to know you are well.

I will be happy just riding with the top down holding on to you until the bell.

I wake with jubilation and sadness deep in my soul but knowing that there is no more pain.

Looking forward to seeing you in my dreams, until we can embrace once again.

Memories

I need a couple more minutes in time.

Just to see two beautiful faces that rhyme.

I want to touch and smell your scent.

Stare in your eyes before your ascent.

Hoping time stands still.

This will make my heart fill.

I speak to you every night from my bed.

You are always in my head.

It's been many years.

But in my mind, it was only yesterday I had tears.

Until we can hold each other to never let go.

And I can say the words that make me glow.

I Love You.

I will always have my precious memories too.

Missing You

I miss you so bad.

I don't see you anymore.

My thoughts always turn to you.

How our lives made perfect rhythm.

When you left, my world was cut to the core.

Why you had to leave, I haven't a clue.

My life is in total mayhem.

My wish is that you were here.

To help calm my fear.

And to keep my world in blissful harmony.

Moving Down The Road

As I move down life's road.

There is so much yakked yak.

It makes me feel as if I got a cold.

It breaks my back from all the attack.

Somedays I stand up and I am bold.

Somedays I feel my life is on track.

That starts the hater's words of lies that unfold.

Never telling the truth or fact.

Believing in the truth about myself that is never told.

I need to keep my mind clear, focused, and intact.

Focusing on my life and to never be controlled.

Letting my family and true friends be my beacon to all the attack.

My Journey

Here I am writing another song that he has put in my head.

I hope someone can relate to keep them on their journey.

Wondering why he puts these words into my head.

I hope the words will loosen the sternest knee.

No matter what life season.

Everyone needs that word or phrase of praise.

For that greater reason.

It is amazing how he shows his ways.

Singing about his happiness and joy.

Don't think the words mean I am an Altar Boy.

Every day my sins I am battling.
Fighting the demons is always challenging.

If just one person can see the love light shine through the clouds.

From these words that have been put under my shrouds.

I am happy the seed was planted.

My Last Ride

Riding in the night I see the universe on high.

It leaves a bright light in the sky.

I see all loved ones that went before.

The first I see are my parents I adore.

I asked my parents did I live my life as they taught.

For all the years I fought.

My dad smiles and hugs me through time and space.

My mom's face is filled with pride as tears rolls down her face.

There are some that would disagree.

For that I have to agree.

I leave my body behind.

My soul is no longer confined.

I hope all I left behind have joy for knowing me.

Instead of sorrow please celebrate with song, laughter, and sweet ice tea.

For the ones that I have hurt I am apologetic.

Please forgive me my life wasn't poetic.

I hope to see you again so we can embrace.

You can see the love I have for you on my face.

After it is over being bitter will never help to see the light.

Know that I never stopped thinking of you through the fight.

Being happy and loved is all you need before the last ride.

My Walk

My walk with the Savior True.

He gives me strength when I'm Blue.

He puts words in my head.

I could have never said.

He speaks to me about many things.

Mostly about the calm and serenity he brings.

We stroll down the path.

He seems to always make me laugh.

I wonder why me?

What does he see?

I only know while he is near.

There is no fear.

My walk with the Savior True.

Near Me

I listen for sounds that you are here with me.

Sometimes the sounds are as simple as a bird's song.

Then other times you come to me in my dreams.

I often wonder how you would deal with the world today.

There are times I am glad you don't have to be here.

There are more times my selfishness wants you here.

My mind can't take much more without you.

Then you remind me that I am stronger than I think.

No matter how many years pass.

There is not a day that I don't think of you.

I listen to hear your voice coming from nature.

I just wait to hear the sound of you, so I know you are by me.

No Take Backs

When you feel that you have no other place to turn.

All your bridges seems like they have been burn.

Stand up straight with your head held high, and know that there is a person in front of you that is aware.

That person will always be there and care.

There will be hands there for support and the strength to carry all your glitches.

Even if you feel all alone know that he will be there for all your hitches.

He knows you better than you know yourself.

He knows your strengths and the weaknesses you possess inside yourself.

All the darkest places in your brain he can bring light.

Look to him to make your whole world bright. Even if you didn't ask, he will be there waiting with open arms no matter how long it takes.

He knows all your pain and suffering, give him all your mistakes.

After you give them to him, never take them back they are not yours anymore.

NOTHING

Can you be happy with nothing?

Can you go through life without an addiction?

We all have needs to have something.

We all have things that give us seduction.

You may not need drugs or alcohol but there is always that thing.

You will always have people that will look at that thing and it will cause friction.

It would be a sad life without love or people that cause that zing.

We are all cursed with some type of affliction.

Let's escape by riding on a snow-white dove's wing.

If you hold a grudge all your life how does that help your conviction?

Will revenge make you feel like a king?

All the wasted time with anger in your heart is like an affliction.

One Day

There will be a day.

I will learn to fly away.

When I get my wings of gold.

All my sins will be paroled.

Embracing the Savior True.

My life's purpose comes into focus and not askew.

All my questions have been resolved.

No more doubt or hate, all has been dissolved.

Only Love and happiness remain.

Glory Glory the Redeemer Reigns.

Pain

When you lose someone, you loved don't let the light in your soul be rebuffed.

You will always have a person holding you up I know it's tough.

Keep your head up and never give up on love.

Never live a lonely life when there is love.

You shared the sun and moon but that doesn't mean there will be darkness.

Open your eyes to see all the love that is still shinning like a big ball of brightness.

Be brave and never close your heart to the beautiful world waiting for your laughter.

Love will be that well-lit corner in your soul that wants to be sought after.

Know that the love in your core will always revitalize your road through time.

There are people who need to look inside to see the light that shines that gives them rhyme.

Share the light from your sun and moon so other may basket in the warmth of love.

PARADISE

We need to stop planning someday.

There is no guarantee that there will be a someday.

Enjoy this day as if were your last day.

Why can't we just live as if the future is today?

Living for tomorrow will never pay.

Always listen to what the elders say.

Live for today and let come what may.

Time is what you never have enough of in a day.

Take that trip that you had planned for one day.

Buy that car you have always wanted with no worries about how you will pay.

Smile, laugh, and dance knowing that everything will be OKAY.

PATH

One night I was dreaming that I was standing in front of my forthcoming.

There were two paths;

The first path was bright with light and smelled of homecoming.

The second path was dark with fire and smelled of decaying excess.

I thought how a life can be changed with a guess.

The first path might seem to be filled with love and hope.

The second could be filled with pain, without a rope.

It is just like seeing someone and judging them for their outward form.

Until you know that person, how can you know their storm.

The difference between Heaven and Hell can be a thin line.

If you choose the path that looks good at the time it may not be fine.

There are always different paths in life, stay on your path.

PERCEPTION

Riding the wave of depression & anxiety.

The pain is real and felt daily.

Some days the wave is too big to ride.

Other days I can maintain my stride.

People think they can tell goods days from bad.

But every day has some bad.

Some wonder why the anxiety & depression?

If that was known, then they wouldn't have the question.

Just because there is not a frown.

Doesn't mean there is not a breakdown.

Just know if I seem standoffish.

It is not my wish.

Try to recognize things are not what they seem.

PLAN

I wish you were still here.

So, you could calm my fear.

I long for your embrace.

And to see your face.

I feel lost.

My mind is suffering the cost.

I run from place to place.

Looking for Saving Grace.

Jesus comes and takes my hand.

Guides me to his plan.

POSITIVE

All that glitters is not the paved road of gold.

Finding yourself when you're not sure you were lost.

Wake up every day hoping there is a better place.

It's time to take control and know that there is a better place.

Believe in yourself and think and say positive things.

Never be satisfied with just fitting it with what life brings.

Reach out and grasp that hand that is always there.

He will always be there in good and bad times without a care.

Give your problems and do not try to take them back.

Always try to live the way He does.

Know that you will fail, but His hand will be there to help you up.

Redbird

I was in my backyard enjoying the day swinging in a hammock.

As I closed my eyes a rush of wind sends me flying through the sky.

While flying above the trees, a couple redbirds started flying beside me on my journey.

As we fly over mountains, several other redbirds began flying with us.

I find myself surrounded as we flew; but instead of fear there is only peace.

Love overwhelms me as I fly blindly protected by the loved ones in the sky.

Soon all the birds began leaving my side and flying in front of me.

As my eyes open; a rush of calmness falls over my soul.

I feel so much joy at this moment knowing love will be guiding me through this life.

Rejoice

Sin is my prison.

Trying to do my best is my vision.

Seems like I will never find. what It is that haunts my mind.

I only have one life.

This life cuts like a knife.

Slices straight to my soul.

Do I disappoint you?

Does it sadden you from your view?

If it's easier to place blame.

Go ahead I will always take the blame.

I feel sad if I ever caused you shame.

I rejoice for the True One that came.

REUNITED

Sometimes I can't remember my own name but I will never forget your face.

As the years roll down this dirt road your memory is just as strong today as it was before.

The only thread of hope is the truth we will be reunited one day with a big embrace,

Seeing everyone that has gone before me, I am falling to my knees for all I adore.

Joy has overcome my being, as we gather together forever in the great unknown.

There are many that I have missed but the sight of my parents makes me humble.

Through all the rejoicing I see the trilogy sitting on the throne.

Feeling that I am home and surrounded by love that will never crumble.

SALVATION

I came for Salvation.

I came for my declaration.

I came for family.

I came for all of humanity.

Teach me how to listen.

Teach me how not to sin.

Teach me how to speak.

Teach me how to seek.

Lead me to your shining light.

Lead me to your everlasting flight.

Lead me to bended knee.

Lead me to the Holy Trinity Three.

Thank you for your gift of Salvation.

Searching

I am an idiot walking thru life with a blindfold.

Never coming out of the cold.

It seems like I have spent my whole life roaming.

Not really knowing who or what I am chasing.

Will I ever settle down and face my fears.

Always burning the candle at both ends.

Never worried about the cost.

Selling out others because I am lost.

Believing all the lies I tell.

Help will not come until I let go of this hell.

I can never feel until I release my loneliness.

Looking into my hearts soul and feeling the calmness.

Don't believe you can never go back home.

I am coming home.

SELF-WORTH

When someone writes you off.

Never write back.

The hard part is not what others think or say.

But not letting their negativity in your mind.

Only fear is holding you back.

Fear that is only in your mind.

Fear that someone has forced in your head.

Negative thoughts from their own fears.

Know your own worth.

It is not arrogance speaking the truth.

If you don't highlight yourself.

Don't expect others to show your light.

Shadows

I always feel there are shadows that follow me.

Are the shadows my mother and father?

Are the shadows my guardian angel?

Or are the shadows something dark and evil?

I feel that there are times it could be a combination of all.

Evil is always trying to whisper in my ear.

Sometime I listen and stumble.

But the other three are there to catch me.

They are always there to clear my path.

Going through life is hard with evil always around the next corner.

I have shadows that will keep me on my path no matter the reason.

Every now and then I stop; close my eyes relax, and talk with the shadows.

Silbling

I am amazed at how the years flew by.

It seems only days ago me and my brother were inseparable.

My two sisters were just a nuisance.

Nowadays I miss them so much I cry.

In my mind our childhood was like a parable.

Being the same as then doesn't make sense.

But my feeling for them just grows stronger with time.

No matter how far we are apart.

There are always things said and done we wish we could erase.

The one thing I never want to erase is being your brother.

Smile

Hello Mama, it's me again.

It's another December without you and Dad.

You think it would get a little easier with the pain.

It still hurts just as bad.

Every day is hard, but this time of year is a strain.

Seems all I feel is sad.

But the thought of you makes me smile.

That makes it all worthwhile.

Soul

I always wondered about people who put demands on their soul.

All the while thinking they are in control.

Always searching for that something.

Empty inside and trying to fill it with nothing.

The weight of the world is on their shoulders.

Never seeing that the weight comes from their own boulders.

The pressure from within is the greatest weight.

The conflict from the outside world and its fate.

Peer pressure is always looming to obtain greater stuff.

Making enough money to pay is always ruff.

Not seeing the hand that is constantly reaching.

Quoting one sentence and thinking they are preaching.

Ease your mind from the guessing.

Let it be well with your soul and all your blessing.

Sounds

I hear the whispers in my ear at night.

Where do the sounds in the dark hide from the light.

The daylight has a different sound than the dark.

Just like good and evil leave a mark.

But which is evil and which is good.

I guess it's like everything only you can take off the hood.

All evil can be twisted into a fairy tale story.

Good can sound mean and gory.

Walk through the dark singing and humming.

Never fear the sounds in the dark, know light is always coming.

When in doubt lay down like the lamb with the lion.

Step By Step

You know the thoughts in my mind.

Help me paint the pictures in my head.

Capture the sunrise and sunsets in my time.

Reach out and touch the brightest stars.

Without you I get lost in the caverns in my mind.

The colors of the day don't shine as bright.

Paint on my brushes set the fight.

With you the paint on the canvas swirls a whimsical shape.

All the beautiful colors of the landscape.

Without you in my present.

There is no future.

Strength

A cup of Coffee Carmel colored sanity.

I am sitting on my front porch reflecting on this exact instant.

Looking over that cup of strength and being able to calm the agony.

The sunlight on my face feels like a warm embrace that is consistent.

With every sip of the mocha madness its peaceful effect sends signals racing.

I need the whole cup to get out of this chair and start pacing.

An empty cup is just like kryptonite to Superman.

I refill my cup with Carmel colored sunbeams.

Hoping this cup gives me the strength to face the outside world.

Struggle

Trying to match how Jesus lived his life.

Always falling to my knees with all my strife.

Knowing my best will always fall short.

Forgiveness is my only hope for my sinful exploit.

Sin can be a prison; the key only Jesus allows.

I am free with Jesus's vows.

Knowing that I am lost in sin.

Letting the blood wash away my sins.

It's hard with the knowledge knowing I will fall.

But I wake everyday giving it my all.

Summer

Feeling the warmth of a Texas summer.

While driving with the top down.

Listening to the sounds of summer.

Hearing nature come alive far from town.

With our favorite song playing on the radio.

Cruising down the back roads, moving slowly with nowhere to go.

My mind is at that crossroads.

Seeing a million stars shining bright.

Thinking it doesn't get any better than this.

Not seeing another set of headlights.

Feeling free, calm, and bliss.

Feeling the warm breeze.

On my face.

Smelling pine trees.

Thankful for having saving grace.

Taking in how Mother Nature has decorated.

Wishing the world was at peace.

So, everyone could soak in the splendor.

In this moment in space.

All is in perfect Harmony.

Listening to Mother Nature's Homily.

Pull over to the side of the road.

So, my mind and body can unite.

My whole being is in Church mode.

Cherishing every moment in this night.

Knowing this second in time will not last.

Always thanking the Savior True.

For the good and the bad in my past.

For all the many ways my Faith grew.

This Texas summer night.

Has made everything right.

THE BOX

I know most will not understand the demon in the box.

The daily struggle to keep the box locked.

When the box is opened, and the struggles begin.

The self-worth and loneliness will start to win.

When others start to question the mood.

Making comments that seem rude.

Only helps the Demon push controversy.

To control your thoughts with no mercy.

I know it's hard to see the possibility.

Through the hostility.

You need to let friends help you seek.

To find the key.

To help with the struggle to keep the box Locked.

Thin Vale

I was walking through a beautiful green meadow.

One spectacular fall orange sunset evening.

I looked across the meadow in the distance stood the Tree of Life.

The tree stood tall and had many colors radiating from its branches.

There were colors emitting from the tree I have never seen.

Beyond the tree there was a magnificent mountain.

At the top of this majestic mountain there was a lighthouse.

The lighthouse was reaching high into the sky.

The light coming from the lighthouse was brilliantly bright.

From a distance I saw what looked like insects flying into the light.

As I walked closer the insects turned into people.

The bright light was showing souls the way home.

It was amazing to see how close life and death were.

I heard voices coming behind me calling my name.

I turned to see who was calling my name.

There was no one, I turned back, and the Tree and

Lighthouse disappeared.

My eyes opened to the sounds of fall.

Back to reality until my name is called.

Thorn

There are days where the same problems persist.

It is easy to blame and create a blacklist.

Is it a thorn in your side?

Or just your foolish pride?

That gives you misery throughout the day.

At times it can be hard to say.

Time is fleeting.

Stop squandering time bleeding.

You never feel like smiling.

When that thorn is reviling.

Problems can be real or in our head.

There are days you don't feel like getting out of bed.

Either real or in your head.

Know that the suffering is real and not just in your head.

Time

Time is the most valuable, precious thing we can never own.

Time truly does march on.

Wasting money, love, friends, and family is devastating.

But wasting time is something that you can never regain.

There will come a day when you ask where has the time gone.

Something that is easy to say but hard to act on.

Live every second as if it were your last.

Don't live in your past.

Have no regrets or enemies, that is a waste of time.

Truth

Day after day I am doing a sleep walk dance.

Everybody wants to spread their thoughts and prance.

I get on a rocket so I can ride fast as the speed of light from sea to shining sea.

You think you know someone but all there is to see is what they want you to see.

People put on that mask of happy smiling faces hiding what is true, because they don't want to go there.

All we hear is others spewing their agendas no matter right or fair.

You think you know what it feels like to be someone else not knowing anything but what you think.

That way of thinking is like seeing a glass full of liquid that looks good so you take a drink.

Always trying to impress worried about what other people think and say.

Not thinking about what is the truth or the price you will pay.

Are we at the point of not caring about thoughts that don't align with the one in our head?

I just want to stop this sleep walk dance and just get back in bed.

Understanding

I might as well be dreaming.

With these words going round and round in my head.

There must be a reason for the ringing.

The words are being led.

The direction is uncertain.

The meaning of the words can be confusing.

Something happens that drops the curtain.

I then understand it not my choosing.

The words flow on the paper.

The writing can end unexpectedly.

My thought vanishes like a vapor.

So, I just wait unpretentiously.

To see when or if more words will lead me.

VIRTUES

One beautiful crisp fall afternoon.

Lying under the dreaming tree.

I found myself talking and strolling with Savior True.

I asked about his greatest Virtue.

He smiled and said just like the Holy Trinity.

The greatest of all virtues, there are three.

Love is one of the three.

Give love with no strings, Love should be given free.

Hope is another virtue to succeed.

Knowing you will fail; hope is that through my blood you will be freed.

Faith is the third virtue.

You are given free will, and still your faith knows that I am the Savior True.

Whispers

It's a wicked thing whispered in the dark.

Making people think that the whispers are truth.

The whispers will start a spark.

Not caring that the whispers are not truth.

It's hard to understand some signs and words are never seen or heard.

While others hear or see hate and believe it to be the true word.

It is hard at times to determine what is true and what is deception.

Whispers try to hide in the dark for deflection.

WICKED

If you are into wickedness you are an evil kind of Troll.

Creating havoc and never paying the toll.

Pilfering what you want with no regard for your soul.

The flames grow higher as you heap in the coal.

Voraciousness is like a drug the more you get the higher you soar.

The smell of the clouds makes you blissful lusting for more.

Not caring who or what stands is in your way.

Just creeping through life for that next fix to bring in the day.

Hiding in the shadows lurking behind walls for the next object of your desire.

Stealing all that you can no matter the cost of family or friends that you throw in the fire.

Building your kingdom is the only thing that commands your lust.

Separating reality from your words and not caring about the trust.

With every conquest you find a way to convince yourself that you are living honorable.

Wickedness will always tell you that you are blameless and others are deplorable.

The foul stitch of greed that fills your soul shows through your total nothingness.

Evil will tell you to avert attention by attacking other with fabrications of foulness.

Wickedness will never let your soul be at peace....

You & Me

I look at you with my googly eyes.

There is no time for lies.

You don't need your witch's spell.

I am willing to tell.

Will you be my guardian angel?

As we travel through the years.

Holding back all the fears.

You have me locked in your jail.

I don't want to fail.

I want to be your bittersweet.

Will you, cherish my love to keep.

Dancing in the dark.

Our bodies held tight makes a spark.

What would be the meaning of life.

If you were not my wife.

DARRELL SOMERS

Darrell Somers is an Artist and Author from Mesquite, Texas. He spent many years ignoring thoughts to start painting and writing.

After painting his first painting in 2011 and writing his first poem in 2017, they became his passion. His paintings are whimsical and his writings are inspirational with a side of whimsy.

His artwork can be seen at Bear Cave Coffee, Flying Squirrel Coffee, Dirty Job

Brewery, Savor Coffee, and Pour Wine Bar, and several other places in the North Texas area.

He graduated from Mesquite High School and achieved his bachelor's degree from Western Governor's University.

You can follow Darrell on Instagram at somers_art

Be sure to check out Darrell's other book "Parents Love" where he shares his thoughts about family, choices and more.

All his books are available at Amazon, Ingram and other online and retail outlets.

www.ingramcontent.com/pod-product-compliance
Lightning Source LLC
Chambersburg PA
CBHW051542120626
46551CB00013B/1343